THE ROMANS

Written by
John Parsons

Deer Run School
Take Home Reading Program
Grade 3

HORWITZ
MARTIN
EDUCATION

Contents

ROMAN NUMERALS

THE LETTERS BESIDE EACH PAGE NUMBER ARE THE ROMAN WAY OF WRITING THEIR NUMBERS. IN ROME, YOU WORKED OUT A NUMBER BY SUBTRACTING OR ADDING LETTERS FROM BEFORE AND AFTER THE LARGEST NUMBER.

I = 1	L=50	M=1,000
V=5	C=100	
X=10	O=500	

ITALY

Campania

Chapter 1

A Mighty Empire

In the year 476, the very last emperor of Rome and his army were defeated in a war against people from northern Europe. The mighty Roman Empire no longer existed. After the war, the emperor, Romulus Augustulus was sent to live in Campania, in the south of Italy.

Once, the Roman Empire stretched from Britain in the west to Syria in the east. It lasted for almost a thousand years. From its capital in Rome, powerful emperors ruled over every country around the Mediterranean Sea. Campania was once a popular holiday place for rich Romans but, by the time that Romulus Augustulus was sent there, it was a quiet seaside farming area. It also had a secret treasure, buried beneath its fields. A complete Roman town, Pompeii, lay under the soil. It would remain hidden until the year 1860.

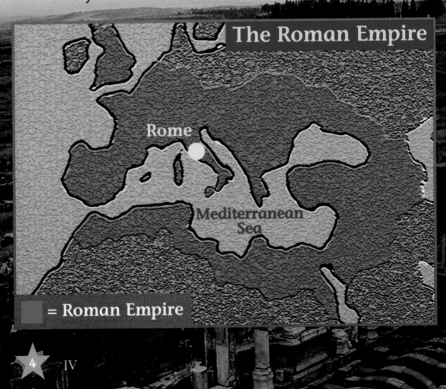

The Roman Empire

Rome

Mediterranean Sea

= Roman Empire

Although the Roman Empire ended over 1,500 years ago, many of the things the Romans invented are still with us today. If you look around, you will see Roman inventions although you might not know it. Concrete, which is used to build the houses and buildings we live and work in, was invented by the Romans. Glass windows, which are in almost every modern building, were invented by the Romans. The letters, and many of the words in this book and everything else you read in English, were invented by the Romans.

So, who were these people we call the Romans? How did they become so powerful? And what terrible thing happened to the town of Pompeii, hidden under Campania where the last Roman emperor lived and died?

Chapter **2**

The Rulers of Rome

There are two different stories about how Rome began. Modern archaeologists, who study the remains of ancient cultures, say that Rome started as a village of small wooden buildings on the hills around the river Tiber in central Italy. But a Roman legend tells a much more interesting story.

The Roman legend tells of twin brothers, Romulus and Remus, who were abandoned as babies. They were rescued by a wolf, who fed and looked after them. When the boys grew up, they decided to build a city in the place where the wolf had discovered them. But they argued, and Romulus killed Remus. Romulus started building the city alone, and it was named after him — the city of Rome. The legend says that the city was started in the year 753 BC.

At first, Rome was ruled by a king. But after two hundred years, the most powerful 100 families formed a group and decided to rule the city themselves. They got rid of their king, and ruled Rome as a group. They were called a Senate, which was an early kind of government. But only members of the most powerful 100 families were allowed to be senators. Ordinary Romans had no say in making the rules.

Ordinary Romans, including most of the Roman soldiers, quickly grew upset at being ruled by the most powerful 100 families. When the Senate realised that the ordinary Romans could easily turn against them, they shared some of their power. Over the next five hundred years, Rome became one of the most powerful cities in the world, and conquered many of the countries in the Mediterranean region.

The success of the early Romans was due to its army. The army was divided into four 'legions', each with about 5,000 soldiers, called legionaries. Each legion was divided into groups of 100 soldiers, called a 'century'. Each century was commanded by an officer, called a centurion. Legionaries rode in chariots and fought with swords, spears, and bows and arrows. They wore metal armour and helmets and brightly coloured tunics. Young Romans joined up to be legionaries for twenty years. During that time, they could share in the treasures that the army captured from its enemies. And at the end of their twenty years, they were given land or money. Being in the army was a good way for ordinary Romans to become rich.

While life in the army was a way to become wealthy, it was also a very harsh life. Roman soldiers were expected to win every battle they fought, and punishment was severe if the soldiers ever ran away from their enemies.

If a group of Roman soldiers ran away, or retreated, from an enemy, they were lined up and every tenth soldier was killed. This punishment was known as being 'decimated'. The name came from 'deca', the Roman word for 'ten'.

The generals who were in charge of the legions grew even richer and more powerful. From about the year 100 BC, the generals, not the Senate, really governed Rome. The senators were too scared to argue with the generals, each of whom had 5,000 soldiers ready to obey their commands. The most famous general was Julius Caesar, who took control of Rome in 49 BC. But the senators were worried that Julius Caesar had too much power, and in 44 BC, he was murdered.

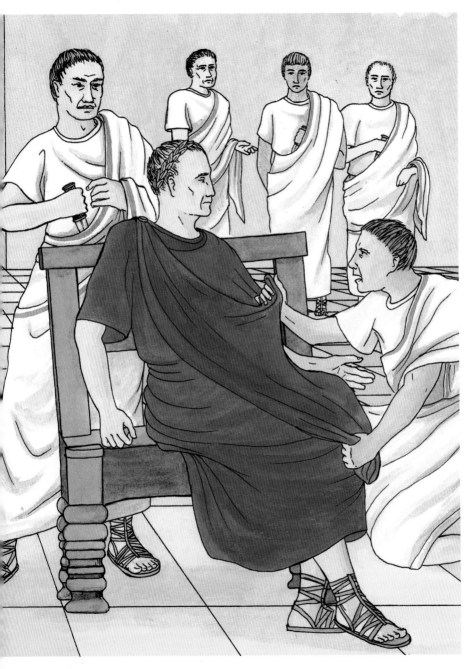

After Julius Caesar, Rome was ruled by two men. One was Julius Caesar's nephew, Augustus. The other was a general called Mark Anthony. At first, they were friends — but things quickly changed!

The Romans wanted to conquer the land of Egypt, which was full of treasures — and, more importantly, was a country that produced lots of wheat. The Romans needed as much wheat as they could find, to feed themselves and their soldiers. Mark Anthony was sent to conquer Egypt with his army, but instead he fell in love with the Egyptian queen, Cleopatra. Together, they plotted to start their own empire. When Augustus heard about this, he sent another army to fight his old friend.

Mark Anthony and Cleopatra lost the battle with the Roman army that Augustus had sent, and Mark Anthony was killed. Cleopatra decided to commit suicide. She allowed herself to be bitten by a poisonous snake, and died before she could be captured by the Romans. Augustus was now the only man in charge of Rome. He became the first in a long line of emperors, who ruled over the Roman Empire for the next five hundred years.

Cleopatra

In between Augustus, who ruled until the year 14 AD, and Romulus Augustulus, who ruled until 476 AD, there were dozens of emperors. Some, like the emperor Nero, were cruel and violent. Others, like Claudius and Vespasian, worked hard to create a fair society. Many men who later became emperors were not even born in Rome. The emperor Hadrian, who built a 116 kilometre stone wall between England and Scotland, was born in Spain.

Chapter 3

Entertainers & Inventors

When it was at its most powerful, the Roman Empire stretched from one end of Europe to the other, and also covered much of North Africa and the Middle East. The land that used to be the Roman Empire is now ruled as thirty different countries. To keep control of such a vast empire, the Romans needed to invent many different ways of transporting food, water, soldiers and messages. At the centre of the empire, Rome became a busy city where over one million people lived. All of them needed food, water, and housing.

The Romans became experts at building things and many structures still stand today. They also had plenty of slaves, captured from the lands they had conquered, to do their work without being paid.

So that their armies could travel long distances, the Romans built thousands of kilometres of roads and bridges. Many of the roads that cross modern Europe and Britain follow ancient Roman roads. The Romans invented concrete to make their bridges and buildings strong and durable. Some bridges, which the Romans called

'viaducts', are still used in France, Spain and Italy. Roman roads were also used by messengers for the world's first postal service, established by the emperor Augustus. People could pay messengers to carry messages almost anywhere in Europe. But because the empire was so big, it often took months before the post arrived.

The million inhabitants of Rome needed huge quantities of water, for drinking, washing and looking after their animals and crops. Nine aqueducts, which were like long canals, were built in Rome. They brought over 1,000 million litres of water from the mountains into the city each day.

The Romans were the first to invent public toilets, and hundreds were built throughout Rome. Up to sixty people at once could crowd into the public toilets, which were often more like meeting places where they could meet friends, and sit and talk while they went to the toilet! Huge sewers were built underneath the city to carry away waste and water.

Hygiene was very important to the Romans, so they built huge and expensive public baths that everyone could use. In the city of Rome, in the year 300 AD, there were 900 public baths. The public baths were like a combination of a swimming pool, a bath and a gymnasium. The best public baths had central heating, powered by huge furnaces underneath the tiled floors. Almost every Roman went to a public bath at least once a day, and they became great meeting places where Romans could socialise and talk about the day's news.

The Romans loved entertainment, and invented many games that children still play today, such as marbles and 'knucklebones'. One of the ways that emperors remained popular was by allowing enormous games events. Special theatres, like the Colosseum in Rome, were built to hold the games. In the games, gladiators would fight each other or hold dangerous chariot races.

During the time of the emperor Augustus, there were almost 10,000 gladiators, who fought each other for entertainment. The possibility that they might be killed was part of the job! One tradition that remains from those days is the 'thumbs up' sign. If a defeated gladiator fought bravely, the emperor would give the thumbs-up sign, which meant that the gladiator should be allowed to live. But if the emperor gave the thumbs-down sign, the gladiator would be killed!

Gladiators also fought dangerous wild animals, such as lions and wolves. While Augustus was emperor, over 3,500 wild animals were killed in battles with gladiators. In later times, Christians were killed and eaten by lions for sport. Until Constantine became emperor in 307 AD, the Romans thought that Christians were enemies of Rome. Then Constantine became a Christian himself!

Before Constantine, the Romans worshipped many different gods. Whenever they conquered a new country, they simply took that country's gods as their own, just in case they were real gods. They also made their emperors into gods as well. Eventually, they had hundreds of gods, with almost seventy different religious festivals every year. The Romans thought that their gods controlled every part of their lives, and they were very superstitious.

For example, the Romans thought that the left side of things was unlucky. A Roman would never put his or her left shoe on first, as it was considered to be very bad luck. The modern word 'sinister', which means bad or evil, comes from the Roman word for 'left'.

Jupiter was the king of the Roman gods, and he was also in charge of the weather. Neptune was Jupiter's brother, and he was the god of the sea. Mars, who was supposed to be the father of Romulus and Remus, was the god of war. Venus was the goddess of love, and Mercury was the messenger of the gods. He wore a winged helmet and sandals. Saturn was a bad-tempered god who was in charge of farming.

NEPTUNE

MERCURY

MESSENGER OF
THE GODS

Many other modern things were invented by the Romans, such as the calendar we use today. At first, they divided the year into ten months, before realising that this wasn't enough. They added two new months — July, named after Julius Caesar, and August, named after the emperor Augustus.

Although a person from ancient Rome might not be able to read this book, he or she would definitely recognise the letters, which come from the Roman alphabet.

Juillet

Septembre

An ancient Roman might recognise some of the words that we use in English. Many of them are Roman words that have changed little over time. And, although we use Arabic numerals for most of our mathematics, they might still see Roman numerals being used in some books and at the end of movies. They might be surprised to know that, even though their empire ended in CDLXXVI, we can still read their numerals in the year MMI!

Chapter **4**

A Sudden End

Even with all the public baths, toilets, sewers, and aqueducts, that were built, Rome was still a crowded, noisy, and smelly city for its million residents. In the city, there were only about 1,800 private homes. The rest of the population lived in huge blocks of flats, up to six floors high. Often, whole families lived and slept in one room. Sometimes, there was nowhere to cook food, so people bought cooked food on the streets or from shops and took it home with them — even takeaway foods are a Roman invention!

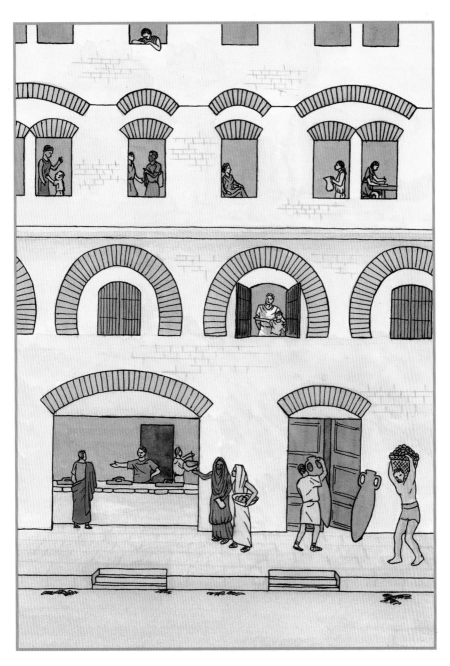

It was no wonder that the richer Romans looked forward to their holidays. In spring and summer, many of the public buildings, such as libraries and law courts, were closed. Life in hot and crowded Rome must have become almost unbearable. Many of the Romans who worked for the government headed south for the summer months. One of the most popular holiday places was the area of Campania where, in later times, the last emperor of Rome would spend his days.

Campania was the area around an ancient city called Neapolis. Neapolis, which is now called Naples, was first built by the Greeks a hundred years before Rome was founded. They also built smaller towns in the area, such as Herculaneum and Pompeii. The first settlers in the area liked the land because it was fertile and they could grow wheat, fruit, vegetables and grapevines there. What they didn't know was *why* the land was so fertile. If they had looked to the east, they would have seen a sleeping volcano called Vesuvius. The ash and mud from ancient eruptions made the soil in the area rich and full of minerals.

Holidays for Romans in Campania were great fun. Wealthy Romans built themselves large holiday homes along the coastline. These holiday homes were decorated with murals, paintings and mosaics. Each house had its own wharf, where the Romans could relax and go fishing. Balconies and windows overlooked the deep blue Mediterranean sea. Nearby, they built temples to whichever gods they thought were most important. Less wealthy Romans could stay in boarding houses in the busy market towns of Pompeii or Herculaneum, and still enjoy their time away from Rome. Pompeii and Herculaneum had all the facilities of Rome, like libraries and public baths — but not the crowds. They were ideal holiday spots.

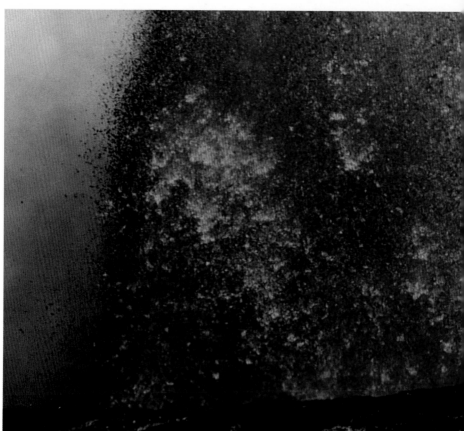

Then, on August 24th, 79 AD, everything changed
for the residents and holiday makers of Pompeii
and Herculaneum. Suddenly, the volcano Vesuvius
erupted, and a massive shower of ash and red-hot
cinders swept over the towns. The eruption was
so violent and so quick that the Romans had no
chance of escape. They were buried under layers of
ash and cinders, along with their homes, gardens,

temples and public buildings. Some families had
enough time to hide in their cellars, underneath
their houses — but they were killed by the poisonous
gases that swept through the town along with the
ash and cinders. Almost 20,000 people were killed
in a few short minutes in Pompeii alone. Life in the
busy Roman towns had stopped suddenly and that
moment in time was frozen for ever.

In the 1860s, an archaeologist named Giuseppe Fiorelli started to excavate the ruins of Pompeii. Under two metres of ash and rock, he found the amazing remains of a busy town. Since then, modern archaeologists have worked to uncover the treasures of Pompeii and Herculaneum. They have carefully removed layer upon layer of ash from the towns, uncovering incredible discoveries. They have found dishes of fruit, nuts and eggs — the remains of meals that were being eaten at the time of the eruption, still sitting in kitchens and dining rooms. They have discovered ovens full of loaves of bread that were being baked on that morning. They have discovered shops, with rows of jars, full of food. They have uncovered beautiful paintings and mosaics on the walls and floors of the mansions of Pompeii, and the contents of houses left just as they were at the time of the eruption.

They have even found the bodies of some Romans, covered in ash where they died on the streets or in their homes. It was like looking at a snapshot of the Roman Empire, taken 2,000 years ago!

Much of what we know about ancient Rome and the Romans comes from the great buildings, roads, waterways, language, and legends that they left behind. But in the ruins of Herculaneum and Pompeii we have found tiny details about the way ordinary Romans lived. The last Roman emperor must have thought a lot about the end of the greatest empire of Europe, as he sat looking over the countryside of Campania. Little did he know that, buried beneath the fertile soil, lay two towns that would give the modern world a glimpse into the way things were when the emperors of Rome ruled the world.

Glossary

ancient cultures
People and a way of life that existed a long time ago.

Arabic numerals
The numbers we use, and the way we write them, today.

archaelogists
Scientists who study the remains of ancient cultures.

armour
Protective metal clothing.

canals
Man-made water-ways.

chariots
Two wheeled, horse-drawn vehicles.

conquered
Took control of, e.g., won a battle to control a country.

defeated
Beaten in a battle.

durable
Strong — lasts a long time.

Empire
A group of countries controlled by an emperor.

excavate
Dig out of the ground.

fertile
Able to grow a lot of healthy plants.

founded
Created or built.

furnaces
Containers that hold a very hot fire.

governed
Ruled, in charge of a town or country.

inhabitants
People who live in a certain place.

region
An area of a country.

severe
Serious — very bad.

society
The group of people who live in a region or country.

superstitious
Believed and feared things that may not be true or real.

tunics
Short sleeved uniforms worn by soldiers.

vast
Extremely large — a great area.

worshipped
Respected, loved and prayed to.

Index